FOOD LOVERS

FISH AND SEAFOOD

RECIPES SELECTED BY MARIKA KUCEROVA

Trans
Atlantic
Press

All recipes serve four people, unless otherwise indicated.

For best results when cooking the recipes in this book, buy fresh ingredients and follow the instructions carefully. Make sure that everything is properly cooked through before serving, particularly any meat and shellfish, and note that as a general rule vulnerable groups such as the very young, elderly people, pregnant women, convalescents and anyone suffering from an illness should avoid dishes that contain raw or lightly cooked eggs.

For all recipes, quantities are given in standard U.S. cups and imperial measures, followed by the metric equivalent. Follow one set or the other, but not a mixture of both because conversions may not be exact. Standard spoon and cup measurements are level and are based on the following:

1 tsp. = 5 ml, 1 tbsp. = 15 ml, 1 cup = 250 ml / 8 fl oz.

Note that Australian standard tablespoons are 20 ml, so Australian readers should use 3 tsp. in place of 1 tbsp. when measuring small quantities.

The electric oven temperatures in this book are given for conventional ovens with top and bottom heat. When using a fan oven, the temperature should be decreased by about 20–40°F / 10–20°C – check the oven manufacturer's instruction book for further guidance. The cooking times given should be used as an approximate guideline only.

CONTENTS

SALMON CURRY SOUP

Ingredients

½ small fresh pineapple

1 small apple

1 banana

1 onion

1 red chili

3 tbsp ghee or clarified butter

1 tbsp curry powder

1 tsp curcuma (turmeric)

4 tbsp coconut milk

475 ml / 2 cups chicken broth (stock)

225 ml / 1 cup milk

Salt and pepper

450 g / 1 lb asparagus spears

350 g / 12 oz salmon fillet

1 tsp lemon juice

Chopped fresh parsley, to garnish

Method

Prep and cook time: 40 min

1 Remove the skin from the pineapple and cut the flesh into small pieces. Peel the apple and cut into small pieces. Slice the banana.

2 Finely chop the onion. Slice the chili into rings, discarding the seeds, and set aside. Heat 1 tbsp of the ghee in a saucepan. Add the onion and fry until softened but not browned. Sprinkle the curry powder and curcuma (turmeric) over the onion and cook for 1 minute.

3 Add the fruit to the onion and heat quickly. Add the coconut milk, broth (stock) and milk and bring to the boil.

4 Remove from the heat and, using a hand-held blender, blend to form a purée. Season to taste with salt and pepper.

5 Cut the asparagus spears into small lengths and cook in a saucepan of boiling salted water for about 5 minutes, until tender but still firm to the bite. Drain and leave to dry.

6 Cut the salmon into bite-sized pieces, drizzle over the lemon juice and season with salt.

7 Heat the remaining 2 tbsp ghee or clarified butter in a non-stick skillet (frying pan). Add the salmon and quickly fry on both sides over a very high heat. Remove from the pan and keep warm. Quickly fry the asparagus in the same pan.

8 Serve the hot soup in small bowls, add the salmon and the asparagus and sprinkle the chili rings over the top. Garnish with parsley.

ASIAN FISH AND NOODLE SOUP

Ingredients

2 swordfish steaks, skinned

1 potato

3 8 scallions (spring onions)

3 2 garlic cloves

1 bird's eye chili

225 g / 8 oz snow peas (mange tout)

1 675 g / 1½ lb egg noodles

Salt and pepper

1 1.2 litres / 5 cups hot vegetable broth (stock)

2 tsp soy sauce

Lime wedges, to serve

Sprigs of fresh cilantro (coriander), to garnish

+ MUSHROOMS
HERBS
TERIYAKI SAUCE
CHIVES

Method

Prep and cook time: 25 min

1 Cut the fish into bite-sized pieces. Finely slice the potato. Slice the scallions (spring onions). Crush the garlic. Very finely slice the chili, discarding the seeds. Cut the snow peas (mange tout) in half diagonally.

2 Plunge the noodles into boiling salted water, cook for 4 minutes, then drain.

3 Meanwhile, pour the broth (stock) into a large saucepan and bring to a simmer. Add the soy sauce, potato, scallions, garlic, chili and fish. Season with salt and pepper and simmer for 5 minutes.

4 Add the noodles and snow peas and warm through for 2–3 minutes.

5 Serve in bowls with lime wedges and garnish with cilantro (coriander).

CATFISH WITH CRESS SAUCE

Ingredients

1 shallot

100 g / 7 tbsp butter

125 ml / ½ cup dry white wine

7 tbsp whipping cream

Salt and pepper

2–3 tbsp cress

2 tbsp lemon juice

4 catfish or rockfish fillets, each weighing about 150 g / 5–6 oz

2–3 tbsp all-purpose (plain) flour

Lemon wedges, to garnish

Method

Prep and cook time: 25 min

1 Chop the shallot. Melt 50 g / 2 tbsp of the butter in a saucepan. Add the shallot and fry for about 1 minute until transparent.

2 Pour in the wine and cook over a medium heat until reduced by about a half. Stir in the cream and season to taste with salt and pepper. Add the cress.

3 Drizzle the lemon juice over the fish fillets. Sprinkle with salt and pepper and dredge with the flour. Shake off any excess flour.

4 Heat 3 tbsp of butter in the pan and fry the fillets over medium heat for 2–3 minutes, on each side, until golden brown.

5 Serve the fish fillets on warmed plates and drizzle the sauce over the top. Garnish with a lemon wedge.

HERB AND GARLIC SHRIMP SKEWERS

Ingredients

2 garlic cloves

12 large raw shrimp (tiger prawns)

Salt and pepper

Grated zest and juice of 2 limes

2 tbsp finely chopped fresh cilantro (coriander)

4 tbsp olive oil

Method

Prep and cook time: 15 min plus 2 hrs marinating

1 Crush the garlic. Put the shrimp (prawns) into a bowl, season with salt and pepper and add the garlic.

2 Add the lime zest and juice, cilantro (coriander) and olive oil and stir together. Cover and chill in the refrigerator for 2 hours to marinate.

3 Preheat the broiler (grill). Thread the shrimp on to 8 wooden skewers. Broil (grill) the shrimp for 5–10 minutes until they turn pink, turning occasionally.

COD FILLETS AU GRATIN

Ingredients

550 g / 1¼ lb floury potatoes

Salt and pepper

2 tomatoes

1 red onion

2 leeks

2 tbsp olive oil

3 tbsp breadcrumbs

3 tbsp freshly grated Parmesan cheese

2 tbsp thinly sliced basil leaves

70 g / 5 tbsp butter, plus extra
for greasing

¼ tsp grated nutmeg

5 tbsp milk

4 cod fillets, each weighing about
150 g / 5–6 oz each

2–3 tbsp lime juice

1 tbsp vegetable oil

Method

Prep and cook time: 1 hr

1 Peel the potatoes, cut into large chunks and put in a saucepan of salted water. Cover, bring to the boil and simmer for about 20 minutes, until tender.

2 Meanwhile, chop the tomatoes, discarding the seeds. Chop the onion and finely slice the leeks. Heat the olive oil in a skillet (frying pan), add the onion and fry until transparent. Add the tomatoes and cook for a further 5 minutes.

3 Remove the onions and tomatoes from the pan and put in a large bowl. Add the breadcrumbs, Parmesan cheese and basil leaves and mix together. Season with salt and pepper and set aside.

4 Heat 25 g / 2 tbsp of the butter in the pan, add the leeks and fry 5–10 minutes until softened.

5 Drain the potatoes, return to the pan and add the milk. Mash until smooth then season with salt, pepper and the nutmeg. Stir in the leeks.

6 Preheat the broiler (grill) to its highest setting. Lightly butter an ovenproof dish.

7 Season the cod fillets with the lime juice, salt and pepper. Heat the remaining butter and vegetable oil in the pan and gently fry the fillets for 2–3 minutes on each side.

8 Place the fish fillets in the prepared dish. Cover with the tomato mixture and broil (grill) for about 2 minutes. Serve on warmed plates with the mashed potatoes and leeks.

WARM SOLE AND SPINACH SALAD

Ingredients

4 tbsp all-purpose (plain) flour

4 fillets lemon sole

2 tbsp olive oil

For the mustard dressing:

4 tbsp olive oil

2 tbsp lemon juice

2 tsp wholegrain mustard

2 tbsp cold water

Salt and pepper

For the salad:

1 scallion (spring onion), chopped

2 eating apples, peeled and cored

150 g / 5 cups baby spinach leaves

Method

Prep and cook time: 30 min

1 To make the dressing, put the olive oil, lemon juice, mustard, water, salt and pepper in a jar with a lid. Cover and shake to mix together. Set aside.

2 To prepare the salad, chop the scallion (spring onion). Peel, core and roughly chop the apples. Arrange the spinach leaves on a serving plate.

3 Spread the flour on to a large plate and season with salt and pepper. Coat the fish fillets in the seasoned flour.

4 Heat the olive oil in a large skillet (frying pan). Add the fish fillets and fry for 4–5 minutes on each side until lightly browned.

5 Serve the sole on top of the spinach and sprinkle over the apples and scallion. Shake the mustard dressing and drizzle over to serve.

SALMON AND LEEK SKEWERS

Ingredients

675 g / 1½ lb salmon fillet

3 red bell peppers

2 leeks

1 garlic clove

Salt and pepper

4 tbsp vegetable oil

2 tbsp rosemary leaves

½ tsp grated zest lemon

Method

Prep and cook time: 20 min

1 Preheat the broiler (grill). Cut the salmon into cubes. Chop the red peppers into bite-sized pieces, discarding the core and seeds. Slice the leeks into 3 cm / 1 inch pieces.

2 Thread salmon, pepper and leek chunks alternately on to wooden skewers.

3 Using the back of a knife, crush the garlic with a little salt. Put in a bowl, add the oil, rosemary and lemon zest and stir together.

4 Brush the oil over the kebabs and broil (grill) for 4–6 minutes, turning several times and basting occasionally with the oil. Season with salt and pepper before serving.

SEAFOOD PAELLA

Ingredients

450 g / 1 lb fresh mussels in shells

350 g / 12 oz prepared squid

1 onion

2 garlic cloves

1 red bell pepper

3 tomatoes

160 ml / 10 tbsp olive oil

1 liter / 4 cups vegetable broth (stock)

8 saffron threads

400 g / 2 cups short grain rice

1 handful frozen peas

300 g / 10 oz peeled shrimp (prawns)

Salt and pepper

2 tbsp chopped fresh parsley

Method

Prep and cook time: 1 hr

1 Preheat the oven to 200°C (400°F / Gas Mark 6). Clean the mussels by scrubbing the shells and pulling out any beards that are attached to them.

2 Roughly chop the squid. Chop the onion and garlic. Chop the red pepper, discarding the core and seeds. Cut the tomatoes in half.

3 Heat 5 tbsp of the olive oil in a large, deep saucepan. Add the onion and fry for about 5 minutes until softened. Add the garlic. Pour in half of the broth (stock) and bring to the boil. Add the mussels and simmer, uncovered, for 10 minutes.

4 Using a slotted spoon, transfer the mussels to a bowl, discarding any that have not opened. Set aside. Put a few spoonfuls of the hot broth in a small bowl. Add the saffron and allow to infuse.

5 Heat the remaining oil in a large paella pan. Add the rice and fry briefly, stirring continuously. Pour in the saffron broth, the onion/broth mixture and the remaining broth. Bring to the boil, stir and simmer for about 15 minutes.

6 Add the red pepper, tomatoes, peas, shrimp (prawns) and squid to the rice.

7 Cover the paella pan with foil and cook in the oven for about 20 minutes. Stir in the mussels 5 minutes before the end of the cooking time, and season with salt and pepper. Sprinkle over the parsley and serve.

MACKEREL WITH DIJON MUSTARD

Ingredients

Butter, for greasing

8 mackerel fillets

2 tbsp Dijon mustard

2 tsp chopped fresh oregano

1 tbsp chopped fresh cilantro (coriander)

1 lemon

2 leeks

4 tbsp olive oil

Method

Prep and cook time: 25 min

1 Preheat the oven to 190°C (375°F / Gas Mark 5). Grease a roasting pan.

2 Make 4 slashes through the skin side of each mackerel fillet. Lay 4 fillets, skin side down, into the roasting pan.

3 Spread the mustard over the flesh of the fillets in the pan and sprinkle a little oregano and cilantro (coriander) over each one. Cut the lemon in half and squeeze the lemon juice over the fillets.

4 Finely chop the leeks and divide them between the fillets. Drizzle over the olive oil and lay the remaining fillets on top.

5 Bake in the oven for 15 minutes until the fish and leeks are tender.

SWEET POTATO AND SHRIMP CAKES

Ingredients

225 g / 8 oz sweet potato

Salt and pepper

200 g / 7 oz canned chick peas, drained

1 small onion

1 garlic clove

450 g / 1 lb peeled cooked shrimp (prawns)

2 tbsp chopped fresh cilantro (coriander)

2 tbsp olive oil

Few sprigs of mint, to garnish

Lime wedges, to serve

For the raita:

10 cm / 4 inch piece cucumber

200 g / scant cup Greek yogurt

2 tbsp chopped fresh mint

For the dip:

2 tbsp sweet chili sauce

1 tsp dark soy sauce

Method

Prep and cook time: 40 min

1 Put the unpeeled sweet potato in a saucepan of salted water, bring to the boil and cook for 10 minutes. Let cool, peel and grate coarsely.

2 Put the chick peas in a food processor and blend until smooth or mash with a fork. Put in a bowl. Finely chop the onion and crush the garlic. Add to the bowl with the shrimp (prawns), sweet potato and cilantro (coriander) and mix together. Season with salt and pepper.

3 To make the raita, finely chop the cucumber and put in a bowl. Add the yogurt and mint and mix together. Put in a serving bowl.

4 To make the dip, stir the sweet chili sauce and soy sauce together and put in a serving bowl.

5 Form the potato and shrimp mixture into patties. Heat the oil in a skillet (frying pan), add the potato cakes and fry over a low heat for 2–3 minutes on each side until browned.

6 To serve, garnish with mint springs and lime wedges and serve with the dip and raita for dipping.

GRIDDLED SQUID BRUSCHETTA

Ingredients

1 garlic clove

1 red chili

450 g / 1 lb prepared squid

8 cherry tomatoes

2 tbsp olive oil

1 tbsp fresh rosemary sprigs, plus extra to garnish

Juice of ½ a lemon

1 ciabatta loaf

4 tbsp garlic mayonnaise

4 little gem lettuce leaves

Salt and pepper

Method

Prep and cook time: 30 min

1 Crush the garlic. Finely slice the chili, discarding the seeds. Slice the tomatoes. Cut the squid into 2 cm / 1 inch pieces.

2 Put the squid in a bowl, add the olive oil, garlic, chili, rosemary springs and lemon juice and mix together. Thread 2 squid pieces on to small wooden skewers.

3 Preheat the broiler (grill) and heat a ridged skillet (frying pan) or griddle pan. Cut the ciabatta bread in half horizontally and then vertically to make 4 pieces. Toast until light golden brown.

4 Spread each piece of toast with 1 tbsp of mayonnaise. Add a lettuce leaf and some sliced tomatoes to each.

5 Season the squid with salt and pepper, add to the hot skillet and cook for 1–2 minutes, turning once, until lightly charred.

6 Serve squid on top of the bruschetta garnished with a few rosemary sprigs.

SPICY SHRIMP SALAD

Ingredients

1 red onion

450 g / 1 lb cherry tomatoes

2 avocados

1 red chili

1 garlic clove

Salt and pepper

8 tbsp olive oil

4 tbsp lime juice

2 tbsp white wine vinegar

450 g / 1 lb cooked peeled shrimp
(prawns)

4 tbsp chopped fresh cilantro
(coriander) leaves

Method
Prep and cook time: 20 min

1 Slice the onion. Cut the tomatoes in half. Cut the avocados into quarters and slice the flesh. Finely chop the chili, discarding the seeds. Crush the garlic.

2 Put all the prepared vegetables into a large bowl. Season with salt and pepper.

3 Pour in the olive oil, lime juice and wine vinegar. Stir in the shrimp (prawns) and cilantro (coriander) leaves and toss together before serving.

SOLE AND SPINACH ROLLS

Ingredients

450 g / 1 lb spinach

40 g / ¼ cup mascarpone

1 tsp lemon zest

Grated nutmeg

Salt and pepper

1 egg yolk

8 sole fillets

1 shallot

40 g / 3 tbsp butter

2 tsp dry vermouth

150 ml / ⅔ cups fish broth (stock)

75 ml / ⅓ cup sparkling wine

75 ml / ⅓ cup whipping cream

Method

Prep and cook time: 45 min

1 Wash the spinach and put in a large saucepan with only the water clinging to its leaves and cook until wilted. Turn into a sieve and drain, squeezing out any excess water.

2 Chop a third of the spinach and put in a food processor. Add the mascarpone and blend to form a purée. Add the lemon zest and nutmeg and season with salt and pepper. Add the egg yolk and mix well together.

3 Spread the spinach mixture over each sole fillet. Roll up and secure with a toothpick (cocktail stick).

4 Finely chop the shallot. Heat 15 g / 1 tbsp of the butter in a saucepan, add the shallot and fry until softened. Add the vermouth and cook until reduced slightly. Add the fish broth (stock) and two-thirds of the sparkling wine and simmer gently for 2–3 minutes.

5 Place the sole rolls into the broth (stock), cover and poach for 4–5 minutes. Remove the fish rolls and keep warm.

6 Strain the cooking liquid through a sieve into a jug. Add half the cream and return to the saucepan. Bring to the boil and cook until reduced by a third. Add the remaining cream and sparkling wine. Season to taste with salt and pepper.

7 Pour about a third of the sauce into a separate pan, add the remaining spinach and warm through.

8 Add the remaining butter to the remaining sauce and, using a hand-held blender, blend until frothy. Serve the sole rolls on the spinach and drizzle over the foamy sauce.

SHRIMP AND ASPARAGUS SALAD

Ingredients

300 g / 10 oz pasta bows

Salt

225 g / 8 oz asparagus

225 g / 8 oz snow peas (mange tout)

7 tbsp plain yogurt

3 tbsp mayonnaise

2 tbsp lemon juice

450 g / 1 lb cooked shrimp (prawns)

2 ripe avocados

1 tbsp chopped fresh dill, to garnish

Method

Prep and cook time: 30 min

1 Cook the pasta bows in a large pan of boiling, salted water according to the packet instructions or until tender but still firm to the bite. Drain, rinse under cold water, and put into a large bowl.

2 Cut the asparagus into 5 cm / 2 inch lengths. Blanch the asparagus and snow peas (mange tout) in boiling salted water for 2 minutes and then drain, plunge into cold water and drain again. Add to the pasta.

3 Put the yogurt, mayonnaise and lemon juice in a bowl and mix together. Stir into the pasta and vegetables. Season generously with salt and pepper. Add the shrimp (prawns).

4 Cut the avocados into quarters and peel away the skin. Remove the stone and slice the flesh. Gently stir into the pasta salad. Spoon into serving bowls and garnish with dill to serve.

TUNA WITH RICE NOODLE SALAD

Ingredients

175 g / 6 oz thin rice noodles

2 tsp sesame oil

2 tbsp soy sauce

1 tbsp chili sauce

1 tsp lime zest

4 tbsp lime juice

1 tbsp runny honey

5 tbsp olive oil

Salt and pepper

3 tbsp sesame seeds

1 red bell pepper

6 scallions (spring onions)

4 tuna steaks, each weighing about 175 g / 6 oz

4 tbsp vegetable oil

1 tsp coarsely ground mixed colored peppercorns

Method

Prep and cook time: 30 min plus 30 min soaking

1 Put the rice noodles in a bowl of warm water and let soak for 30 minutes to soften. Drain well, put in a bowl and stir in a little of the sesame oil.

2 To make the dressing, put the soy sauce, chili sauce, lime zest and juice, honey, remaining sesame oil and 3 tbsp of the olive oil in a large bowl and mix together. Season with salt.

3 Toast the sesame seeds in a dry non-stick skillet (frying pan). Remove from the pan and let cool.

4 Thinly slice the red peppers, discarding the core and seeds. Thinly slice the scallions (spring onions).

5 Heat the remaining olive oil in the pan, add the red peppers and fry for 3–4 minutes. Add the scallions and fry for a further 2 minutes. Season with salt. Add the hot vegetables to the dressing. Add the toasted sesame seeds and mix together.

6 Season the tuna steaks with salt and pepper. Heat the vegetable oil in the pan and fry the steaks on each side for 2–3 minutes.

7 Serve the tuna topped with the noodles and vegetables and sprinkle with coarsely ground pepper.

COD WITH TOMATO AND OLIVE CRUST

Ingredients

2 tbsp olive oil, plus extra for greasing

4 cod fillets

100 ml / 7 tbsp dry white wine

1 onion

2 garlic cloves

150 g / 1/3 cup pitted (stoned) black olives

12 pieces sun-blushed tomatoes, drained from oil

1 tbsp chopped fresh parsley

Method

Prep and cook time: 35 min

1 Preheat the oven to 180°C (350°F / Gas Mark 4). Grease an ovenproof dish.

2 Put the fish fillets into the dish and pour in the wine.

3 Chop the onion, garlic cloves and olives. Put in a bowl, add the sun-blushed tomatoes, parsley and olive oil and mix together.

4 Spread the tomato and olive mixture on top of the fish fillets.

5 Bake in the oven for 20 minutes until the fish flakes easily. If wished, serve with green (French) beans and roasted cherry tomatoes.

SEAFOOD SPAGHETTI

Ingredients

115 g / 4 oz string (runner) beans

Salt and pepper

450 g / 1 lb spaghetti

1 small onion

4 garlic cloves

2 tbsp olive oil

675 g / 1½ lbs mixed prepared seafood, thawed if frozen

125 ml / ½ cup vegetable broth (stock)

150 g / ⅔ cup crème fraîche

2–3 tbsp lemon juice

50 g / ½ cup grated Parmesan cheese

Basil leaves, to garnish

Method

Prep and cook time: 30 min

1 Cook the beans in a saucepan of boiling salted water for about 10 minutes until tender but still firm to the bite. Rinse under cold water and drain well.

2 Meanwhile, cook the spaghetti according to the instructions on the packet.

3 Chop the onion and garlic cloves. Heat the oil in a large saucepan, add the onion and garlic and fry for 2–3 minutes. Add the seafood and fry for a further 2–3 minutes.

4 Pour in the vegetable broth (stock) and bring to a boil. Stir in the crème fraîche. Reduce the heat and season with the lemon juice, salt and pepper. Stir in the beans and reheat them.

5 Drain the spaghetti and mix with the seafood sauce. Serve on warmed plates sprinkled with the Parmesan cheese. Garnish with the basil leaves.

GARLIC MUSSELS WITH CHORIZO

Ingredients

2 kg / 4½ lbs mussels

1 large onion

200 g / 7 oz chorizo

2 garlic cloves

Olive oil for frying

475 ml / 2 cups dry white wine

Pepper

Fresh parsley sprigs, to garnish

Method

Prep and cook time: 30 min

1 Clean the mussels by scrubbing the shells and pulling out any beards that are attached to them.

2 Roughly chop the onion. Remove the skin from the chorizo and roughly chop. Chop the garlic. Heat the olive oil in a large saucepan, add the onion and fry for 2–3 minutes, until softened.

3 Add the chorizo and cook for 2 minutes. Add the garlic and cook for a further 2–3 minutes.

4 Add the mussels, pour in the wine and season with pepper. Cover the pan, bring to the boil then cook over a medium heat for 5 minutes, until the mussels open.

5 Using a slotted spoon, discard any mussels that have not opened. Serve garnished with parsley.

TUNA SKEWERS WITH COUSCOUS

Ingredients

675 g / 1½ lb tuna fillet

2 cm / ¾ inch piece fresh ginger

Juice of 1 lemon

2 tbsp vegetable oil

Juice of 1 orange

2 tbsp honey

Lemon wedges, to garnish

For the couscous:

250 g / 1⅓ cups couscous

1 carrot

2 cm /1 inch piece fresh ginger

1 onion

2–3 tbsp toasted slivered (flaked) almonds

3–4 sprigs roughly chopped fresh parsley

2 tbsp butter

3 tbsp raisins

Juice of 1 orange

About 1 tbsp garlic oil

Salt and pepper

Method

Prep and cook time: 40 min plus 30 min marinating

1 Cut the fish into cubes. Peel and grate the ginger. Put the ginger, lemon juice and oil in a large bowl. Add the fish and put in the refrigerator for 30 minutes to marinate.

2 Thread the fish on to wooden skewers. Reserve the marinade.

3 To prepare the couscous, cook the couscous according to the packet instructions. Grate the carrot, grate the ginger and finely chop the onion.

4 Heat the butter in a saucepan, add the carrot, ginger and onion and cook until the onion is translucent. Add the slivered (flaked) almonds and raisins, stir in the orange juice and bring to the boil briefly. Add garlic oil to taste and season with salt and pepper.

5 Add the onion mixture and parsley to the couscous. Let stand then check the seasoning.

6 Meanwhile, preheat the broiler (grill) and broil (grill) the fish kebabs until tender, turning several times.

7 Put the reserved marinade and orange juice into a small pan. Bring to the boil and boil until reduced by half. Stir in the honey.

8 To serve, spoon the couscous on to warmed serving plates, add the fish kebabs and sprinkle over the sauce. Garnish with lemon wedges.

FISH CURRY

Ingredients

1 small can pineapple chunks

225 g / 8 oz cherry tomatoes

450 g / 1 lb white fish fillets

2 tbsp lemon juice

Salt and pepper

1 tbsp red curry paste

375 ml / 1²/₃ cups coconut milk

150 ml / ²/₃ cup plain yogurt

1 tsp corn starch (cornflour)

25 g / 1 cup shredded fresh basil

1–2 tbsp light soy sauce

8 chives, to garnish

For the rice:

Butter, for greasing

200 g / 1 cup basmati rice

Salt

Method

Prep and cook time: 40 min

1 Drain the pineapple chunks, reserving the juice in a jug. Roughly chop the pineapple. Slice the tomatoes in half.

2 Cut the fish into bite-size pieces, discarding any bones. Sprinkle the lemon juice over the top and season with salt and pepper.

3 Cook the rice according to the instructions on the packet. Lightly butter 4 individual molds.

4 Meanwhile, heat the oil in a wok, stir in the curry paste and fry briefly. Add the coconut milk, bring to the boil, and then simmer for 2 minutes. Stir in the pineapple chunks.

5 Mix the yogurt with the corn starch (cornflour) until smooth and add to the wok.

6 Pour in 150 ml / ²/₃ cup of the reserved pineapple juice and bring to the boil. Season with the soy sauce.

7 Add the fish pieces and tomatoes and bring to the boil. Cover, turn off the heat and allow to poach for 2–3 minutes. Stir in the basil.

8 Divide the rice equally into the prepared molds. Turn the rice out of the molds on to warmed plates. Serve the curry next to the rice and garnish with chives, if wished.

COD AND VEGETABLE GRATIN

Ingredients

1 tbsp butter, plus extra for greasing

4 cod fish fillets, each weighing
175 g / 6 oz

3 tbsp lemon juice

225 g / 8 oz carrots

225 g / 8 oz leeks

1 tbsp all-purpose (plain) flour

225 ml / 1 cup milk

¼ tsp sugar

¼ tsp grated nutmeg

1 tbsp medium hot mustard

½ tsp curry powder

Salt and pepper

2 tbsp crème fraîche

1–2 tbsp chopped fresh parsley

Method

Prep and cook time: 1 hr

1 Preheat the oven to 190°C (375°F / Gas Mark 5). Lightly grease an ovenproof dish with butter.

2 Sprinkle the fish with the lemon juice and leave to rest for 5–10 minutes. Finely slice the carrots and leeks.

3 Melt the butter in a saucepan. Stir in the flour and cook until the flour begins to brown. Add the milk gradually, using a whisk to blend the milk with the flour and butter mix.

4 Bring the sauce to a boil and then simmer for 10 minutes. Add the sugar, nutmeg, mustard and curry and season to taste with salt and pepper. Remove from the heat and stir in the crème fraîche.

5 Put the carrots and leeks in the prepared dish, arrange the fish pieces on top and sprinkle with the parsley. Pour over the sauce.

6 Bake in the oven for 25–30 minutes until the fish is tender.

SPAGHETTI WITH MUSSELS

Ingredients

1 kg / 2 lb 4 oz fresh mussels in shells

450 g / 1 lb cherry tomatoes

1 onion

4 garlic cloves

150 ml / 2/3 cup white wine

Salt and pepper

450 g / 1 lb spaghetti

2 red chilies

2 tbsp olive oil

Salt and pepper

2 tbsp chopped fresh chives, to garnish

Method

Prep and cook time: 40 min

1 Clean the mussels by scrubbing the shells and pulling out any beards that are attached to them. Put in a large saucepan with a cupful of water. Cover with a tight fitting lid and cook for 3–4 minutes until the mussels open.

2 Using a slotted spoon, transfer to a bowl, discarding any mussels that have not opened. Strain the cooking juices and reserve.

3 Cut the tomatoes into quarters. Chop the onion and crush the garlic. Add the tomatoes, onion, garlic and wine to the pan, bring to the boil and simmer for 5 minutes.

4 Meanwhile, bring a large pan of salted water to the boil. Add the spaghetti and cook for about 10 minutes, or according to the packet instructions, until tender but still firm to the bite.

5 Finely slice the chilies, discarding the seeds. Add the chilies, oil, spaghetti and mussels to the tomato mixture and toss together. Season with salt and pepper and serve garnished with chopped chives.

Published by Transatlantic Press

First published in 2011

Transatlantic Press
38 Copthorne Road, Croxley Green, Hertfordshire WD3 4AQ

© Transatlantic Press

Images and Recipes by StockFood © The Food Image Agency

Recipes selected by Marika Kucerova, StockFood

A catalogue record for this book is available from the British Library.

ISBN 978-1-908533-66-1

Printed in China